GIANTS AND DEMONS

Kumbhakarna the Sleeping Giant

SHUBHA VILAS

Om Books International

Once Ravana, his younger brothers Kumbhakarna and Vibhishana, and their sister Surpanakha, performed penance to please Lord Brahma.

The four of them did tapasya for many years till Brahma appeared before them.

Ravana asked for immortality. Then Brahma turned towards Kumbhakarna to ask what boon he desired. Kumbhakarna was prepared with his answer. He wanted Indrasan (throne of Indra) as a boon from Brahma.

Brahma knew that the demon would want something like that. He was prepared. He had asked Saraswati Devi, the goddess of learning, to help him utter the right words. Sure enough, Saraswati Devi intervened and manipulated Kumbhakarna's speech.

Kumbhakarna then ended up asking for Nidrasan (boon for sleep) instead of Indrasan! As he heard himself speak, Kumbhakarna was aghast. He definitely did not want to sleep for the rest of his life.

Kumbhakarna pleaded with Brahma to undo the boon. Showing compassion, Brahma relaxed his boon. From now on, instead of sleeping all the time, Kumbhakarna would sleep for six months and remain awake for the next six months.

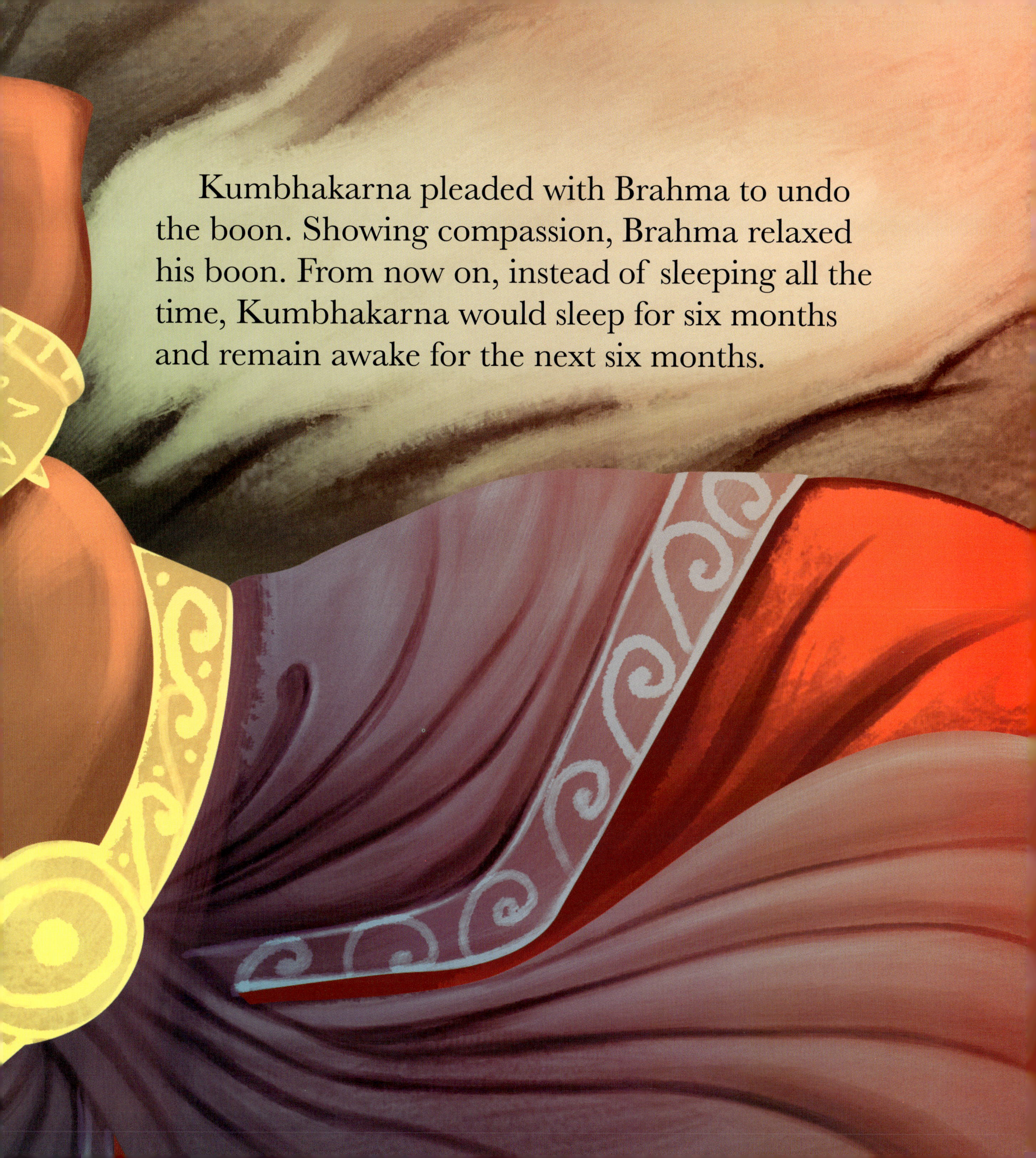

To wake him up after six months of sleep, many men would create a loud noise for hours. Elephants, horses, donkeys, all together trumpeting, neighing and braying. Then followed trumpets, bugles and conches and also drums, gongs and bells.

Finally they had to poke him with tridents, arrows and swords. With all this, and much more, he would stir a little. After he awoke, it took him several hours more to get into complete action. Finally, with a huge yawn, he would angrily demand food. Hundreds of cartloads of all varieties of food were brought to him and he gobbled all of it in a hurry. After a few hours of non-stop eating and drinking, Kumbhakarna would finally wake up.

Even though Kumbhakarna spent half his life sleeping, Ravana trusted him more than his life. When he was fighting a losing battle with Shri Rama, Ravana turned to Kumbhakarna for help.

Kumbhakarna showing his loyalty, said, "Though you were totally wrong, as a brother I will stand by you. Whoever Rama and Lakshmana may be, and however powerful they may be, I will destroy them. I will kill Rama even before his second arrow reaches me. I will also kill their entire monkey army. O brother, you can now relax and enjoy."

A confident Kumbhakarna went all alone to the battlefield to defeat Lord Rama. He created panic by gobbling up many monkey soldiers. He captured the monkey king Sugriva, who bit off his ears and nose. Rama then shot arrows at him, chopping his hands and legs. Soon, his mountainous body fell down and Kumbhakarna breathed his last.